C000235870

101 Electric P
Cooker Recipes

By

Liana Green

www.LianasKitchen.co.uk

My Amazon Author Page:

www.amazon.co.uk/Liana-Green

www.amazon.com/Liana-Green

DISCLAIMER

Although the author and publisher have made every effort to ensure that the information in this book was correct at press time, the author and publisher do not assume and hereby disclaim any liability to any part for any loss, damage, or disruption caused by errors or omissions, whether such errors or omissions result from negligence, accident or any other cause.

INTRODUCTION

Pressure cookers are currently seeing a resurge in popularity since their heyday during the 20th century. I'm sure many of us born during the 70's and 80's will remember the scary sounding pressure cooker, hissing away on the stove, threatening to spurt out its contents if you went within 3 foot of it.

Thankfully the current renaissance of the pressure cooker has brought about the development of electric pressure cookers, a much quieter, and more importantly, safer appliance from those of yesteryear.

Benefits of Using a Pressure Cooker

Although using a pressure cooker for the first time may seem daunting and overwhelming, once you get used to this method of cooking, you will soon begin to appreciate the many benefits and wonder how you ever managed without it in your kitchen.

- Create delicious and nutritious meals in a shorter time.
- Vegetables retain more of their vitamins and nutrients when prepared in a pressure cooker.
- Save on food costs. Cooking under pressure allows you to use tougher and cheaper cuts of meat. The end result will be a tender yet nutritious meal without having to wait hours for it to cook.
- Create a variety of meals with a versatile pressure cooker. You can stew, fry, boil, bake, steam and sauté in a pressure cooker.
- Save on appliances and cookware. A good multi cooker should mean you can replace many of your kitchen pots and gadgets, and simply use the one appliance.
- Save on fuel consumption when compared to a conventional oven or stove-top
- Less heat in the kitchen. A sealed pressure cooker will release minimal heat and steam.

Which Pressure Cooker Should I Use?

Options include the popular electric pressure cookers, often packaged up as multi-cookers with claims to do just about everything in your kitchen, aside from the washing up. Instant Pot has led the way with multi-cookers, developing a huge following of dedicated fans. The Instant Pot is an excellent choice of electric pressure cooker, as are other brands, in particular, the Pressure King Pro.

And if you prefer to stick to the traditional stove-top pressure cookers, you can't go far wrong with any models from the well known brands including Tefal, Tower, Prestige and VonShef.

The Recipes in This Book

All the recipes in this book have been tried and tested using an Instant Pot. However, they are suitable for all types of pressure cookers, just make sure you have read and understood any particular recommendations in the manual that came with your model.

Whilst you shouldn't have any problems with the recipes in this book, on rare occasions things might not turn out quite right. It can be something as simple as an incorrectly measured ingredient, or a different make of ingredient used. Whatever the reason, if you want any help, or have any questions, please feel free to contact me at liana@lianaskitchen.co.uk I'm more than happy to assist, and if I don't know the answer, I can usually find out!

How a Pressure Cooker Works

When pressure is increased the temperature at which liquid boils will increase accordingly. Because a pressure cooker is a sealed environment, the steam cannot escape as it would in a pan on the stove. The steam essentially cooks the food - which is why it is important to have adequate liquid levels in your pot.

Liquid Levels

I cannot stress enough how important it is to have the minimum liquid requirements in your cooker before you attempt to pressure cook anything. Without enough liquid, there won't be enough steam to reach pressure, and to stay at pressure. The result of this could be uncooked food, and worst still, scorched food.

The Instant Pot advises you have at least 1 cup of water which should be a good rule of thumb for most models (but do check with your manufacturer). The good news is, this doesn't all need to come from water alone. It can be from stock, vegetables, meats, wine etc.

Pressure Cooker Lingo

Quick Release (QR)

When a recipe calls for a quick release, sometimes written as QR, this means you should manually bring down the pressure as soon as the cooking time has finished. On an electric pressure cooker like the Instant Pot, this involves moving the steam release handle to the venting position. This will enable the steam to be let out until the float valve drops down. Once the float valve has dropped down you can take the lid off your pressure cooker.

Always take care when using this method of release as the steam coming out will be very hot. Keep hands and other body parts out of the way. If you prefer, you can use a wooden spoon or spatula to knock the handle into the correct position.

Be careful using this method on recipes with large amounts of liquid or foods high in starch.

Using the quick release method is useful when you want to stop the cooking process quickly to avoid over cooking, especially ingredients such as vegetables.

Natural Release (NR)

A natural release is when you leave the pressure cooker to do its thing on its own. If you don't intervene at all your machine will automatically go into this mode. Natural release usually takes anywhere from 10 minutes and upwards, depending on what ingredients and liquid levels you have inside.

You can speed up the natural release process by covering the pot in a damp towel.

A natural release is best used when cooking large cuts of meat to allow them adequate resting time. It is also recommended to use this method when cooking beans and pulses. They have a tendency to foam up which could potentially escape through the steam valve and block it.

A good compromise is to allow a 10 minute natural release, followed by a quick release.

Pot In Pot

Sometimes abbreviated to PIP, Pot In Pot basically means using another cooking pot or container within the pressure cooker pot. Usually the 'pot' is rested on a trivet. The pot can be made out of any material that is suitable for use in an oven such as silicone, ceramic, stainless steel etc.

Sling

Sometimes it can be hard lift your dish out when using the pot in pot method. It's not only awkward, it's also hot. A brilliant way round this is to make your own sling. You can make it out of a tea towel or some foil. I prefer to use foil as the tea towel will get all wet and soggy. Unroll and lay out about 50cm of foil and fold it into a strip about 5cm in width. This is what you will use to lower and lift any pot in and out of your pressure cooker.

Quick Tips

- **Invest in some herbs and spices.** Many of the recipes in this book, in fact, in many pressure cooker recipes; you will find the need to add herbs or spices. Just a tiny dash of spice can make all the difference to an otherwise bland dish.
- **If you want a thicker sauce** you will need to use the simmer/sauté/heat function on your pressure cooker at the end of cooking, with the lid off. In some cases just 5 minutes will make all the difference. It will also enhance the flavour of your dish. If you are short on time, other options include adding cornflour, flour or stirring in some cream.
- **Watch how much you put in your cooker.** Although there might seem to be a lot of space in your pot, don't fill it by more than two thirds full, and for recipes that include beans, grains, fruit and rice, not more than half way (they will expand as they cook). Your cooker needs enough space for the steam to circulate.

Converting a Recipe

Many recipes can be adapted for a pressure cooker. Recipes that need liquid or steaming when cooking are ideal for conversion. Even baked recipes can be made in a pressure cooker.

Most conventional recipes need to be reduced in cooking time by two thirds. So a recipe that would take 60 minutes on the stove or in the oven should only take 20 minutes in a pressure cooker. However, always check the recommended cooking times for each ingredient and consider that items such as vegetables might need to be added later in the cooking process to avoid over cooking.

The best kind of meats to use in a pressure cooker are the cheaper cuts, often the tougher and fattier ones.

Other Equipment You Might Need

Trivet - most electric pressure cookers come with a trivet, if not, they are quite cheap to buy. Trivets are used when you need to raise a dish above the water level and steam it.

Steamer Stand/Basket - ideal for cooking fish, vegetables and eggs in.

Loaf Tin - any oven proof one is suitable, as long as it fits ok in your pressure cooker pot.

Spare Sealing Rings - the silicone sealing rings in electric pressure cookers tend to retain the smell of whatever has been cooked in there, not ideal when you make a lot of curries as well as cakes and bakes. It's worth having a separate silicone sealing ring for spicier recipes.

MAKING STOCK

Stock features in many pressure cooker recipes. Although it is perfectly fine to use shop bought stocks, you might choose to make your own from time to time.

Thanks to the pressure cooker, it's not as hard as you think!

You can make stock ahead of time and store it in a refrigerator for up to 5 days, or freeze it for up to 4 months. Store stock in useful measured out volumes, such as in 250ml increments. That way, when you are ready to make a soup, you can take one or two out and just top up with some more water if required.

You can add your own vegetable peelings such as that from carrots, celery, parsnip etc to add to your stock. It will all be sieved before use.

If you can, keep the bones and carcasses from your own meals and use these to make your stock. Store meat bones in the freezer until you have enough to make a stock. Or alternatively, ask at your local butchers for some.

You can spice up stocks by adding in chillies, ginger and other spices and herbs.

VEGETABLE STOCK

Makes approx 2.5 Litres

1 large onion, quartered
2 medium carrots
2 parsnips
1 medium tomato
4 sticks celery
3 cloves garlic (unpeeled)
2 bay leaves
1 tsp pepper
1 tsp salt
2 tsp mixed herbs
Water

1. Add all the ingredients, unpeeled, to your pressure cooker pot. Add enough water to cover them, taking care not to go over the maximum fill level.

2. Cook at high pressure for 15 minutes and allow pressure to release naturally.

3. Strain the stock through a sieve (a piece of muslin might be useful to line the sieve with).

4. Store the stock in airtight containers and keep in fridge, or freeze for later.

Tip: Add in what vegetables you want to according to your tastes and seasonal availability.

CHICKEN STOCK

Makes approximately 2.5 litres of stock

1 large chicken carcass (or 2 small ones)
2 onions, unpeeled and quartered
2 celery sticks, chopped
2 carrots, chopped
2 garlic clove, chopped
1 bay leaf
Sprig of thyme
8 black peppercorns, lightly crushed
Water

1. Add all the ingredients to a large pot and cover with water, taking care not to go over the maximum recommended fill level.

2. Cook in high pressure for 30 minutes. Allow a natural pressure release.

3. Strain the stock through a sieve (a piece of muslin might be useful to line the sieve with).

4. Store the stock in airtight containers and keep in fridge, or freeze for later.

BEEF STOCK

Makes about 2.5 litres of stock

1.3kg beef bones (from cooked joints)
2 onions, unpeeled and cut into quarters
2 celery sticks, chopped
1 medium tomato
2 carrots, chopped
1 bay leaf
1tsp dried thyme (or other dried herbs)
8 black peppercorns, lightly crushed
200ml red wine
Water

1. Place the bones into a large roasting tin with the carrot, onion and tomato. Roast for around 30 minutes, until the bones have darkened.

2. Transfer the bones and vegetables to the pressure cooker pot. Add the herbs, wine and enough water to cover the vegetables, keeping under the maximum recommended fill levels. 3. Cook at high pressure for 40 minutes. Allow a natural release.

4. Strain the stock through a sieve (a piece of muslin might be useful to line the sieve with). 5. Skim off any fat that has settled on the surface.

6. Store the stock in airtight containers and keep in fridge, or freeze for later.

FISH STOCK

Makes approx 2.5L of stock

1kg fish bones and trimmings (from white fish)
1 onion, unpeeled but chopped
1 celery stick, chopped
2 carrots, sliced
3 garlic cloves, unpeeled
1 bay leaf
8 black peppercorns, crushed
200ml white wine
Water

1. Make sure the fish bones and any other trimmings you are using are rinsed thoroughly.

2. Add everything to the pressure cooker pot and cover with water, taking care not to go over the maximum fill level.

3. Cook at high pressure for 12 minutes and allow pressure to release naturally.

4. Strain the stock through a sieve (a piece of muslin might be useful to line the sieve with).

5. Store the stock in airtight containers and keep in fridge, or freeze for later.

CHICKEN MAINS

SWEET & SOUR CHICKEN

Serves 4

2tbsp vegetable oil
4 chicken breasts, diced
1 red pepper, sliced
1 medium onion, sliced
400g tin pineapple chunks in juice
2tbsp cornflour

For the sauce
½ tsp Worcestershire sauce
100g tomato ketchup
2tbsp brown sugar
60ml soy sauce
60ml apple cider vinegar (or white wine vinegar)
2 cloves garlic, crushed

1. In a mixing bowl or jug, stir together all the sauce ingredients.

2. In the pressure cooker pot, heat the vegetable oil and sauté the onions for 5 minutes.

3. Add the chicken and gently cook for a few minutes until the meat is sealed.

4. Add the peppers and pineapple (including the juice). Switch off the sauté function.

5. Pour in the sauce from step 1. Cook at high pressure for 3 minutes and then allow to release naturally for 5 minutes before manually releasing.

6. Remove the lid and switch on the sauté function. Whisk the cornflour with a little water (or according to packet instructions) and add to the mixture. Stir until thickened.

Serving Suggestion: Serve with rice or noodles.

CHICKEN IN PEANUT SAUCE

Serves 4

4 tbsp vegetable oil
3 tbsp clear honey
4 chicken breasts
1 tbsp ground coriander
3 garlic cloves, crushed
2 tbsp curry paste
2 tbsp brown sugar
3 tbsp smooth peanut butter
400ml coconut milk

1. In a separate bowl mix together 3 tbsp vegetable oil, the honey, ground coriander and crushed garlic cloves. Spread this mixture over the chicken breasts and leave to marinate for 20 minutes.

2. Heat 1tbsp vegetable oil in the pressure cooker pot. Add the peanut butter, curry paste and brown sugar and sauté for 2 minutes. Add the coconut milk and continue to heat until the mix begins to boil.

3. Switch off the sauté function and add the marinated chicken to the pot.

4. Set to high pressure for 4 minutes. When finished, do a quick release.

5. Remove the chicken from the pot and shred with a fork. It should come apart easily as it will be nice and tender.

6. Return the shredded chicken to the pressure cooker pot and stir into the sauce. Switch the sauté function off.

Serving Suggestion: Serve with rice or noodles.

CHICKEN TIKKA MASALA

Serves 4

4 chicken breasts
1 tbsp olive oil
1 medium onion, chopped
4 garlic cloves, crushed
1tbsp grated ginger/1tsp ground ginger
4tbsp tikka masala powder (or to make your own, see below)
300g passata
150ml chicken stock
150ml double cream

1. Heat the olive oil in the pressure cooker pot and sauté the onions and garlic for 3 to 4 minutes, or until soft.

2. Add tikka masala spice mix and continue to sauté for a further minute.

3. Add the chicken breasts and gently seal on both sides. You may need to add a little chicken stock to deglaze the bottom of the pot.

4. Add the passata and chicken stock and allow to come to a gentle boil.

5. Switch off the sauté function and set to high pressure for 7 minutes. Quick release when finished. Switch to sauté function.

6. Leave the sauce to boil down and thicken up a little. During this time remove the chicken from the pot and shred with a fork. It should come apart easily as it will be nice and tender.

7. Return the shredded chicken to the pressure cooker pot and stir into the sauce. Switch the sauté function off.

8. Stir in the double cream. You don't need to use all the double cream, just until you reach your desired creamy texture.

Serving Suggestion: Serve with rice and naan bread.

Tikka Spice Mix

2tsp garam masala

3tsp coriander

3tsp cumin

2tsp chilli

1tsp garlic powder

1tsp turmeric

1tsp ginger

Pinch of salt

Simply mix all of the above ground spices together and add to the recipe. If you want to make up a batch of tikka spice mix you can double/triple/quadruple this recipe and store the rest for another time.

SIMPLE THAI RED CURRY

Serves 4

4tbsp Thai Red Curry Paste
1 tbsp olive oil
4 chicken breasts
400ml coconut milk
Juice of 1 lime
4 garlic cloves, crushed
1 red pepper, deseeded and sliced
1 onion, sliced
1 red chilli, sliced (optional for extra kick)

1. Heat the oil in your pressure cooker pot. Add the onion and garlic. Sauté for 3 to 4 minutes.

2. Add the chicken breasts and gently sear on both sides.

3. Add the Thai red curry paste and ½ the coconut milk. Allow to come to a gentle boil.

4. Add the rest of the coconut milk, peppers, lime juice and red chilli. Stir to mix in. Switch off the sauté function and cook on high pressure for 7 minutes. Once finished quick release the pressure and remove the lid. Switch to sauté function.

5. Remove the chicken breasts from the pot and using a fork shred them.

6. Return the shredded chicken to the pot and gently heat for a few more minutes.

7. Serve with rice of your choice.

Suggestion: If you have some, add in mange tout and baby sweet corn at step 4.

THAI CHICKEN & NOODLES

Serves 4

4 - 6 boneless chicken thighs
115g (4oz) egg noodles
2 tbsp olive oil
5cm (2inch) fresh root ginger, peeled and finely sliced
2 garlic cloves, crushed
1 red chilli, deseeded and finely sliced (leave seeds in for a hotter taste)
1 fresh lemongrass
½ tsp turmeric
1 can coconut milk
600ml chicken stock

1. Heat up the pressure cooker on sauté for 1 minute.

2. Add the oil and heat for a further 30 seconds.

3. Add the chicken thighs. Allow the chicken to seal and brown for approximately 3 minutes on either side. Use tongs to turn over.

4. Remove the chicken and place to one side on a plate.

5. Add 100ml of the chicken stock and deglaze the pot.

6. Add the ginger, chilli, garlic, lemongrass and turmeric and cook for 2 minutes.

7. Switch off the sauté feature

8. Add the coconut milk and the remaining chicken stock

9. Place the chicken thighs back in the pressure cooker.

10. Place the lid on and manually set on high pressure for 7 minutes.

11. You can choose to either cook your noodles in a separate pan whilst the chicken is cooking, or you can wait to cook them in the mixture at the end. I prefer the taste of them in with the mixture as well as giving it the opportunity to allow the sauce to thicken up a little.

12. Allow the pressure cooker to naturally release for 3 minutes before quick releasing it.

13. If cooking the noodles now, take off the lid and press the sauté button. Add the noodles and cook for 3 to 4 minutes or according to pack instructions. Stir continuously.

Recipe Tip: If you prefer a thinner more soup like consistency, add more stock during stage 13.

TROPICAL CHICKEN

Serves 4

1kg boneless chicken thighs
50g olive oil
1 large onion, chopped
1 x 340g tin pineapple cubes in syrup
250ml chicken stock
2tsp ground ginger
1 tbsp desiccated coconut
1 tbsp Worcestershire sauce
2 tsp cornflour

1. Heat the olive oil in the pressure cooker pot. Add the chicken thighs and gently brown. Add the onions to the pressure cooker and gently sauté for 2 to 3 minutes. Remove the chicken and onion from the pressure cooker and set aside.

2. Switch off the sauté function and drain out any fat from the pressure cooker pot.

3. Add the tin of pineapple (including the syrup), ginger, Worcestershire sauce and stock to the pressure cooker. Mix together.

4. Return the chicken and onion to the pot.

5. Cook at high pressure for 5 minutes and then reduce pressure using a quick release.

6. Remove the chicken from the pressure cooker. Switch on the sauté function with the sauce still in there.

7. Stir the cornflour with a little cold water until blended together (or according to packet instructions) and mix in to the pressure cooker. Allow to cook until desired consistency has been reached. Remember to continue stirring during this time.

8. Pour the sauce over the chicken.

Serving Suggestion: Serve with rice or noodles.

SPANISH CHICKEN ONE POT

Serves 4

1tbsp vegetable oil
4 boneless chicken thighs
375ml chicken stock
1tsp ground turmeric
350g long grain rice, rinsed
1 green pepper, chopped
50g chorizo, diced
3 garlic cloves, minced
1 medium onion, chopped

1. Add the ground turmeric to the chicken stock and set to one side.

2. Switch pressure cooker on into sauté mode. After 1 minute, add vegetable oil and allow to heat. Add chicken and brown on both sides for around 5 minutes. Remove from the pot and set aside on a plate.

3. With the sauté button still on, add the chopped onions and allow to cook for 3 to 5 minutes or until they start to soften.

4. Add the pepper, chorizo and garlic and stir round. Allow to cook for 1 to 2 minutes.

5. Add a swig of chicken stock and deglaze the pan.

6. Add the rice and mix. Sauté for a further minute.

7. Switch off the sauté button and add the remaining stock in. Add the chicken thighs.

8. Place the lid on and put on manual high pressure for 6 minutes.

9. Allow natural release for 10 minutes and then perform a quick release.

CHICKEN RICE CASSEROLE

Serves 2-4

½ tbsp olive oil
2 chicken breasts, cubed
10 mushrooms, diced
190g wild rice, rinsed
60g double cream
250ml chicken stock
¼ tsp salt
¼ tsp garlic powder

1. Heat oil in pressure cooker pot.

2. Add all ingredients to pot and stir to mix down into liquid

3. Cook on high pressure for 23 minutes, and natural pressure release.

CHICKEN, SAUSAGE, SWEET POTATO AND BRUSSEL SPROUT CASSEROLE

Serves 4

2 tbsp olive oil
2 chicken breasts, cubed
2 large sausages, sliced
3 large sweet potatoes, cubed
350g frozen brussel sprouts
¼ tsp salt
¼ tsp pepper
¼ tsp basil
¼ tsp thyme
125ml chicken stock

1. Sauté chicken cubes and sausage together in oil until cooked.

2. Add spices to pot and stir.

3. Add stock, potatoes and brussel sprouts and stir.

4. Cook on high pressure for 3 minutes; naturally release pressure for 5 minutes. Manually release carefully, a little steam at a time.

HOT LEMON CHICKEN

Serves 4

4 chicken breasts, sliced into strips
60ml lemon juice
60ml water
1 tbsp sherry
2 tbsp manuka honey
¼ tsp garlic powder
¼ tsp cayenne
¼ tsp salt

1. Put lemon juice, water, sherry, honey, and spices in pot. Heat on warm until honey is dissolved.

2. Add chicken to pot. Cook high pressure 8 minutes, and natural pressure release 10 minutes, before quick release.

CHICKEN CHICKPEA CASSEROLE

Serves 4

4 chicken breasts
1 large onion, diced
1 tbsp olive oil
150g dried chickpeas
2 x 400g cans of chopped tomatoes
375ml chicken stock
½ tsp salt
¼ tsp pepper

1. Sauté onion in oil until tender (about 4-5 minutes).

2. Add chicken, chickpeas, tomatoes, stock and salt and pepper. Make sure chicken is submerged in liquid. Cook on high pressure for 45 minutes and natural pressure release.

TURKEY MEATBALLS

Serves 4

500g minced turkey
125g parmesan cheese
30g flour
1 medium egg, beaten
Pinch salt
Pinch pepper
¼ tsp garlic powder
¼ tsp ground ginger
1 tbsp olive oil
Sauce of choice (try Thai Sweet Chilli Sauce) OR 225g passata and 120ml water

1. Add all ingredients to bowl. Mix well until combined.

2. Form into small, equal sized balls

3. Heat olive oil on sauté and add meatballs a few at a time, browning on all sides.

4. Add sauce of choice and all meatballs to pot.

5. Cook on low pressure for 10 minutes, and quick pressure release when done.

BEEF MAINS

BOLOGNESE

Serves 4

1tbsp olive oil
500g beef mince
400g (tin) passata
400g (tin) chopped tomatoes
1 medium onion, chopped
2 cloves garlic, crushed
1tsp mixed dried herbs
1tbsp tomato puree

1. Heat the oil in the pressure cooker pot. Add the onion and garlic and sauté for 3 to 4 minutes.

2. Add the mince and gently cook until browned.

3. Add the remaining ingredients and stir.

4. Switch the sauté function off and set to cook at high pressure for 15 minutes. Allow to release naturally for 10 minutes before releasing manually.

Serving Suggestion: Serve with spaghetti, or on a baked potato.

BEEF GOULASH

Serves 4

2 tbsp olive oil
600g stewing steak
2 tbsp plain flour
1 onion, chopped
1 red pepper, sliced
100g pancetta
3 garlic cloves, crushed
2tbsp ground paprika
1 tbsp mixed herbs
2 tbsp tomato puree
400g tin plum tomatoes
250ml beef stock
150ml soured cream

1. Toss beef in flour and paprika.

2. Heat oil in pressure cooker pot. Add onion and garlic and sauté for 3 to 4 minutes.

3. Add bacon and beef and gently cook for 2 to 3 minutes.

4. Add a little beef stock to deglaze the pot.

5. Add the herbs, puree, tomatoes, pepper and remaining stock. Switch off the sauté function.

6. Put the lid on the pressure cooker and set to high pressure for 10 minutes. Allow to release naturally for 5 minutes before releasing manually (quick release).

7. Remove lid and stir in the sour cream.

Serving Suggestion: Serve with mashed or boiled potato.

BEEF BURRITOS

Serves 4

2 tbsp vegetable oil
500g beef mince
1 onion, chopped
2 cloves garlic, crushed
1tbsp dried oregano
2 tsp ground chilli
2 tsp ground paprika
2 tsp ground cumin
2tbsp fresh coriander leaves
400g tin chopped tomatoes
200ml beef stock
8 flour tortillas
125g grated cheese

1. Heat the oil in the pressure cooker pot. Add the onion and garlic and sauté for 3 to 4 minutes or until soft.

2. Add the paprika, chilli, oregano and cumin. Stir in for 1 minute.

3. Add the beef mince and cook for around 5 minutes, or until browned.

4. Switch off the sauté function. Add the tomatoes and stock.

5. Cook at high pressure for 20 minutes and then release pressure quickly (quick release).

6. With the lid off, sauté/heat until the sauce thickens or reduces to preferred consistency.

7. Divide the mixture between the 8 tortillas and roll up and fold over (you may need to use a cocktail stick to secure them in place). Place tortilla parcels in a baking tin or dish. Sprinkle grated cheese over the top and place under a grill for a few minutes to allow cheese to melt.

Serving Suggestion: Serve with sour cream and salad.

PEPPERED MEATLOAF

Serves 4-6

200g minced beef
200g sausage meat
100g sage and onion packet mix
1 green pepper, deseeded and finely sliced
2tbsp tomato puree
30ml water
1 egg, beaten

You will also need: Lightly greased loaf tin and trivet.

1. Using a large mixing bowl, combine all the ingredients, binding it together with the beaten egg.

2. Transfer the mixture to the greased loaf tin and push it down and level it out.

3. Cover the tin with baking paper or foil.

4. Add 375ml of water to the pressure cooker pot. Place a trivet inside the pot and lower the dish on top of the trivet. You may want to use a folded tea towel or foil as a makeshift sling as discussed in the introduction.

5. Cook at high pressure for 30 minutes. Reduce pressure quickly (quick release).

6. Gently lift the loaf tin from the pressure cooker, carefully taking off the paper or foil cover. 7. Turn the tin upside down to remove the meatloaf.

Serving suggestion: Tastes great served warm as part of a main meal or cold served with salad or in a lunch box.

CHILLI CON CARNE

Serves 4

2tbsp olive oil
500g lean minced beef
1 onion, chopped
2 garlic cloves, crushed
1tsp ground paprika
1tsp ground cumin
1tbsp chilli powder
400g tin of red kidney beans, drained
150ml beef stock
400g chopped tomatoes
1tbsp Worcestershire sauce
1 bay leaf

1. Heat oil in pressure cooker pot and sauté onion and garlic for 3 to 4 minutes.

2. Add the mince and cook until lightly browned.

3. Add the paprika, cumin and chilli powder, heat for 30 seconds.

4. Switch off the sauté function and add the kidney beans, beef stock, chopped tomatoes, Worcestershire sauce and bay leaf.

5. Set to high pressure for 10 minutes. Allow a natural release for 10 minutes before manually releasing.

Serving Suggestion: Serve with rice or on a baked potato.

BEEF BOURGUIGNON

Serves 4-6

750g braising/stewing beef
40g flour
1 tsp salt
1 tsp pepper
2 tbsp olive oil
100ml sherry
375ml beef stock
3 medium carrots, sliced to 2-inch sticks
1 small onion, chopped
4 garlic cloves, sliced thin

1. Add flour, salt and pepper to a sealable plastic food bag. Seal and shake to mix.

2. Add beef cubes to bag a few at a time and shake to coat meat.

3. Heat oil on medium sauté and brown cubes of beef in inner pot a few at a time, removing cubes to plate as browned, until all cubes are removed.

4. Press cancel to start cooling the pot.

5. Add sherry to pot, scraping against bottom to lift all brown bits.

6. Return meat to pot and all remaining ingredients.

7. Cook on high pressure for 23 minutes, and quick pressure release when done.

Serving Suggestion: Serve over egg noodles.

TACO MEAT

Serves 4-6

500g minced beef
1 tbsp olive oil
1 onion, diced
5 garlic cloves, crushed
1 tsp salt
1/4 tsp cayenne
1 tsp chilli powder
2 tsp cumin
1 tsp cocoa
125ml beef stock
70g oats

1. Heat the oil in the pressure cooker pot and gently sauté the onion and garlic for about five minutes.

2. Add spices and sauté for 1 minute more.

3. Add minced beef and sauté until brown.

4. Stir in beef stock and oats.

5. Cook on high pressure for 10 minutes, and natural pressure release for 15 minutes, before releasing remaining pressure.

Tip: This makes a mild, sticky taco meat, perfect for serving in shells and flavouring with other fresh onion, peppers and vegetables. For a spicier meat, double the cayenne and chilli powder.

NACHO BEEF AND BEAN TOPPING

Serves 4

450g minced beef
2 tbsp olive oil
1 onion, chopped
5 garlic cloves, crushed
1 red chilli pepper, finely sliced
1 yellow chilli pepper, finely sliced
1 tsp salt
$\frac{1}{4}$ tsp cayenne
$\frac{1}{4}$ tsp black pepper
1 tablespoon cumin
1 tsp paprika
1 can black beans, with juice

1. Heat oil in pressure cooker pot. Gently sauté the onion, garlic and chilli peppers until all are tender.

2. Add spices and sauté for 1 minute more.

3. Add the beef mince to the pot and stir until all meat is broken apart and mostly cooked.

4. Add beans with juice to pot, stir in.

5. Cook on high pressure 10 minutes, and natural pressure release.

Serving Suggestion: Serve over nachos with your choice of toppings. Choose from melted cheese, salsa, guacamole, sour cream, or a bit of everything!

ALMOST ROAST BEEF

Serves 4

450g stewing beef, cubes cut in half
125ml apple cider vinegar (or vinegar of your choice)
125ml water
5 garlic cloves, 2 crushed, 3 whole
½ tbsp olive oil
8-12 new potatoes
4 medium carrots, chopped
2 whole large onions
¾ tsp salt
¼ tsp pepper
250ml beef stock

1. Combine the vinegar, water, 2 crushed garlic cloves, and ¼ tsp salt in a bowl. Submerge the stewing beef in the bowl and allow to marinate 20-30 minutes.

2. Whilst the meat is marinating, prepare the vegetables for the pressure cooker pot. The new potatoes and onions can go in whole.

3. Put the marinated meat, 3 whole garlic cloves, potatoes, carrots, onions, salt and pepper, and stock in the pot.

4. Cook on high pressure for 12 minutes, allow it to naturally release for 5 minutes, then manually release.

LAMB

LAMB SHANKS IN RED WINE

Serves 4

4 lamb shanks
4tbsp olive oil
1tsp ground cinnamon
1tsp ground cumin
1tsp ground coriander
1 green chilli, finely chopped (remove seeds for a milder taste)
2 large tomatoes, chopped
3 cloves of garlic, crushed
2 onions, chopped
2 carrots, chopped
100ml vegetable stock
250ml red wine
1tbsp tomato puree
Chopped parsley for garnish (optional)

1. Heat 2 tbsp olive oil in the pressure cooker pot. Gently brown and seal the lamb shanks. You might need to do this 2 at a time, depending on sizes.

2. Remove all lamb shanks from the pot and set aside on a plate.

3. Add the remaining 2tbsp olive oil and add the onions, carrots and garlic. Gently sauté for 3 to 4 minutes.

4. Add the cinnamon, cumin and coriander and mix together for 30 seconds.

5. Add the tomatoes and green chilli. Cook for a further minute.

6. Add a little vegetable stock to deglaze the pot if necessary.

7. Add the rest of the stock, tomato puree and red wine. Allow to come to the boil before switching off the sauté function.

8. Place the lid on and set to high pressure for 30 minutes. Let pressure release naturally.

9. If the sauce is too thin, stir in some cornflour or thickening granules.

10. Optional: sprinkle fresh, chopped parsley across the top.

Serving Suggestion: Serve with mashed potato and green veg.

LAMB KEEMA

400g lamb mince
2 tbsp vegetable oil
1 onion, chopped
2 cloves garlic, crushed
1 cinnamon stick
8 peppercorns
1 tbsp fresh root ginger, grated (or 1tsp ground ginger)
3 cloves
2 fresh green chillies, finely sliced
½ tsp ground turmeric
½ tsp garam masala
1 tsp ground cumin
400g crushed tomatoes
100g frozen peas

1. Heat the oil in the pressure cooker pot. Gently sauté the onions and garlic for 2 to 3 minutes. Add the cloves, cinnamon and peppercorns and gently cook for a further 30 seconds.

2. Add the lamb and gently cook it until lightly browned. Add the ginger, chillies and spices and stir in.

3. Add the crushed tomatoes and stir in.

4. Switch off the sauté function and put the lid on the pressure cooker. Cook at high pressure for 10 minutes and release quickly (quick release).

5. Remove the lid and add the frozen peas. Set the pressure cooker to the sauté function and stir through for 3 to 4 minutes.

Serving Suggestion: serve with rice or baked potato.

LAMB CURRY

Serves 4

**1 tbsp olive oil
1 onion, chopped
400g diced lamb
2 tbsp mild curry powder
1 tsp chilli powder
375ml lamb stock (or vegetable)
2 tbsp tomato puree
50g raisins or sultanas**

1. Heat the oil. Add the chopped onion and sauté until it begins to colour.

2. Add the lamb and cooked until starting to brown.

3. In a separate bowl stir together the curry powder, chilli powder and tomato puree. Add this mix to the lamb and onion and gently sauté for a further minute.

4. Switch off the sauté function and stir in the hot stock and raisins.

5. Cook at high pressure for 15 minutes.

6. Perform a quick release. If the sauce needs to be thickened a little either sauté it with the lid off or add some cornflour and stir in.

Serving Suggestion: Serve with couscous or rice.

LAMB AND GUINNESS STEW

Serves 4

1kg lamb shoulder, cut into cubes
1tbsp olive oil
2tbsp tomato puree
1 medium onion, chopped
3 cloves of garlic, crushed
1tsp dried mixed herbs
1tbsp mustard
1tbsp Worcestershire sauce
4 medium carrots, chopped
200g frozen peas
200ml lamb or beef stock
250ml Guinness or any other stout or ale

1. Heat the oil in the pressure cooker pot. Gently brown the lamb; this may need to be done in two parts to avoid overcrowding. Set the lamb aside.

2. Add the onion and garlic and gently sauté for 4 to 5 minutes, until they start to soften.

3. Add a little of the stock to the pot and scrape off any stuck bits on the bottom.

4. Add the remaining ingredients, including the lamb but not the peas. Stir to combine.

5. Turn off the sauté function and set to high pressure for 15 minutes. Allow a natural release.

6. Switch to the sauté function and add the frozen peas. Stir through and gently simmer for 5 minutes to allow the peas to cook through and the sauce to thicken a little.

Serving Suggestion: Serve with crusty bread or mashed potato.

PORK

PORK & APRICOT RIBS

Serves 4

1 tbsp olive oil
750g pork spare ribs
1 small onion, chopped
1 x 400g apricot halves
250ml chicken/vegetable stock
2 tbsp Demerara sugar
2 tbsp wine vinegar
2 tbsp Worcestershire sauce
1 tbsp tomato puree
1tsp mustard powder
1 tbsp cornflour

1. Heat the oil in the pressure cooker pot. Add the onion and gently sauté for 2 to 3 minutes before adding the pork spare ribs. Cook the pork until lightly browned.

2. Add the onions and sauté for 2 to 3 minutes.

3. Add the juice from the apricot halves and the stock. Stir.

4. Add the sugar, vinegar, Worcestershire sauce, tomato puree and mustard powder.

5. Cook on high pressure for 15 minutes. Reduce pressure quickly (quick release).

6. Switch the pressure cooker to the sauté function. Mix the cornflour with a little water and stir it in. Once the sauce has thickened, add the apricot halves and allow to heat through.

Serving Suggestion: Serve with rice.

PORK, APPLE AND CINNAMON

Serves 4

1 tbsp olive oil
4 pork chops
1 medium onion, chopped
1 cinnamon stick
2 celery sticks, chopped
200ml clear apple juice
150ml vegetable stock
1 cooking apple, cored and cut into quarters
1 bay leaf
1 tbsp clear honey

1. Heat the oil in the pressure cooker pot. Add the onions and lightly sauté for 2 to 3 minutes.

2. Add the pork chops and brown, a few minutes on each side should be enough.

3. Add the chopped celery, cinnamon stick, apple juice, vegetable stock, honey, bay leaf and cooking apple. Gently mix together.

4. Cook at high pressure for 10 minutes. Allow to release naturally for 5 minutes before manually releasing (quick release).

Serving Suggestion: Serve with mashed potato and vegetables of your choice.

GINGER AND ORANGE GAMMON

Serves 4 to 6

1kg boneless gammon joint
3 carrots, chopped
5 peppercorns
5 cloves
1 bay leaf
1 orange, sliced

For The Glaze
6tbsp orange marmalade
1tsp ground ginger
2 oranges

1. If the joint is smoked soak it in cold water for at least 6 hours. If you don't have time, place the joint in the pressure cooker and bring to the boil using the sauté/heat function. Leave to stand for 5 minutes. Drain and discard the liquid.

2. Place the gammon joint in the pressure cooker pot. Cover with cold water taking care not to go over the maximum three quarters full rule.

3. Add the carrots, cloves, peppercorns, sliced orange and bay leaf.

4. Cook at high pressure for 16 minutes (8 minutes per 500g).

5. Reduce pressure quickly (quick release)

6. Take the joint out of the pressure cooker pot and leave to one side to stand.

7. Preheat the oven to 200C/Gas Mark 6

8. **Making the glaze:** In a bowl mix the marmalade, ginger and juice from the oranges.

9. Remove any rind left on the gammon (be careful if it is still very hot).

10. Using a sharp knife, score lines in the gammon. Spread the glaze over the gammon.

11. Place the glazed gammon in a suitable casserole dish and cook for 15 minutes.

Serving Suggestion: Serve with fried egg and chips. Use any leftovers for sandwiches or cold lunches.

PAPRIKA PORK

Serves 4

2tbsp vegetable oil
1 medium onion, chopped
600g pork fillet/tenderloin, cut into 4cm cubes
2tbsp paprika
300ml vegetable stock
3tbsp white wine vinegar/sherry
1 red pepper, thinly sliced
150ml soured cream

1. Heat the oil in the pressure cooker pot and sauté the onion for 2 to 3 minutes.

2. Add the pork fillet and lightly brown, approximately 5 minutes.

3. Stir in the paprika and cook for a further minute.

4. Add the stock and wait for it to boil before turning off the sauté function.

5. Add the sherry and red pepper.

6. Cook at high pressure for 8 minutes and leave to release naturally for 10 minutes before manually releasing (quick release).

7. Stir in the soured cream.

Serving Suggestion: Serve with rice or mashed potato.

SEAFOOD

MANGO CHERRY SALSA WITH FISH

Serves 4

Fresh white fish or salmon, 4 pieces
1 tbsp coconut oil
½ onion, chopped
1 apple, cored and chopped
300g mango chunks, fresh or frozen
125ml cherry juice

1. Heat coconut oil in pressure cooker pot. Sauté onion and apples for about 3 minutes.

2. Add mango chunks and cherry juice to pot. Stir.

3. Nestle fish into fruit, and cook on high pressure for 3 minutes for thinner fish, and 4 minutes for thicker fish.

Serving Suggestion: Serve over coconut rice.

TUNA CASSEROLE

Serves 4

1tbsp olive oil
100g dry pasta
180ml vegetable stock
1 x 160g can tuna
¼ tsp salt
⅛ tsp pepper
¼ tsp paprika
¼ tsp sage
¼ tsp basil
⅛ tsp garlic powder
125g cheddar cheese, grated

1. Heat oil in pressure cooker pot.

2. Add stock, pasta, spices and tuna. Stir.

3. Cook on high pressure for 2 minutes. Quick release.

4. Serve with cheese sprinkle on top. Melt under a grill if required.

SWEET AND SOUR SCALLOPS

Serves 6-8

36 scallops
100g blackberry (or black currant) jam
100g apricot (or peach) jam
100g mustard
2 tbsp water

1. Add blackberry jam, apricot jam, mustard and water to the pressure cooker pot. Mix well.

2. Press scallops into sauce to ensure they are covered completely.

3. Cook at high pressure for 3 minutes. Quick pressure release.

GARLIC PRAWNS

400g raw prawns
3 tbsp olive oil
3 tbsp salted butter
5 garlic cloves, sliced thin
80ml lemon juice
80ml dry sherry
1 tsp paprika
1 dried red chilli pepper, crushed
2 tsp salt
⅛ tsp pepper
1 tbsp fresh parsley, shredded (optional)

1. Heat the oil and butter on warm until butter fully melts.

2. Add all ingredients, except the prawns to the pot. Stir to combine.

3. Pat prawns dry and place in a steamer basket in the pressure cooker pot. Keep the prawn out of sauce, or the sauce will be too heavily flavoured by the prawns.

4. Cook at high pressure for 2 minutes, natural pressure release for 10 minutes, and then manually release remaining steam.

5. Pour sauce over prawn in a bowl.

VEGETARIAN MAINS

AUBERGINE AND TOMATO CURRY

Serves 4

2 aubergines, diced
2 tbsp salt
4 medium tomatoes, diced
3tbsp olive oil
1 medium onion, chopped
3 cloves garlic, crushed
2 bay leaves
1tsp ground cumin
1tsp ground coriander
1tsp ground chilli
1tsp ground turmeric
125ml vegetable stock

1. Optional: Place aubergine in a colander over a bowl and sprinkle the salt over, ensuring it is distributed throughout. Leave for 30 minutes. Wash with cold water and pat dry aubergine with paper towel. This helps to remove some of the potentially bitter taste of the aubergine.

2. Heat the oil in your pressure cooker pot. Add the onions and aubergine Sauté on a gentle heat for 5 minutes. Add the crushed garlic and spices. Sauté for a further minute.

3. Switch the sauté feature off and add the tomatoes, stock and bay leaves.

4. Cook at high pressure for 3 minutes. Quick release.

Serving Suggestion: Serve with rice or a potato dish.

SPICED VEGETABLE CASSEROLE

Serves 4

2tbsp olive oil
2 medium carrots, finely sliced
1 red pepper, finely sliced
4 sticks celery, finely sliced
1 medium onion, chopped
1tsp cinnamon
1tsp paprika
1tsp ground ginger
1 small cauliflower, cut into florets
1 red pepper, sliced
25g raisins (optional)
125ml vegetable stock
400g tin chopped tomatoes
1tsp apple cider vinegar
100g cheddar cheese, grated

You Will Also Need: Heatproof casserole dish

1. Heat the olive oil in your pressure cooker pot. Add the carrot, onion, celery, pepper and garlic. Gently sauté for 2 to 3 minutes.

2. Add the paprika, ginger and cinnamon. Stir well to combine and sauté for a further 2 minutes.

3. Add the cauliflower, raisins (if using), chopped tomatoes, vinegar and stock. Switch off the sauté function.

4. Set to high pressure for 4 minutes and then quick release.

5. Transfer to a suitable heatproof dish. Sprinkle with cheese and brown off under a grill.

BUTTERNUT SQUASH RISOTTO

Serves 4

500g butternut squash, peeled & diced
2tbsp vegetable oil
1 medium onion, sliced
2 garlic cloves, crushed
400g Arborio rice
700ml vegetable stock
100ml dry white wine
1tsp dried thyme
100g parmesan cheese, grated
40g butter

1. Heat the oil in the pressure cooker pot. Sauté the onion and half the butternut squash for around 5 minutes.

2. Add the rice and sauté gently for a further 2 minutes.

3. Add the wine and scrape off anything that has stuck to the base of the pot.

4. Add the stock, remaining butternut squash and dried thyme. Cook at high pressure for 5 minutes. Quick release.

5. Stir the rice round for some time to soak up and absorb any water. If the rice seems too watery still, switch on a gentle heat and cook until whilst stirring until the preferred consistency is achieved.

6. Stir in the cheese and butter until melted.

COURGETTE RISOTTO

Serves 4

1 tbsp vegetable oil
200g Spanish rice/Arborio rice
1 onion, chopped
1 red pepper, deseeded and chopped
1 (approx. 500g) courgette, chopped
2 garlic cloves, crushed
400g tin chopped tomatoes
250ml vegetable stock

1. Heat oil and sauté onion for about 4 to 5 minutes

2. Add pepper and continue to sauté for a further 3 minutes

3. Add courgette, rice and garlic and sauté for 1 minute

4. Add a little vegetable stock to deglaze if required

5. Switch sauté off and add remaining vegetable stock and chopped tomatoes

6. High pressure for 4 minutes

7. Natural release for 10 minutes. If the risotto is too watery, sauté for a short while

PENNE PASTA IN TOMATO SAUCE

Serves 4

340g penne pasta
450g pasta sauce (see <u>Tomato Pasta Sauce</u> recipe under <u>Sauces and Dips</u> or use a jar)
1 tbsp olive oil
1 red pepper, chopped
1 medium onion, chopped
2 cloves garlic, crushed
250ml water*
120ml double cream
50g parmesan cheese, grated

1. Heat oil up in pressure cooker pot.

2. Add chopped onion and garlic and sauté for 4 to 5 minutes.

3. Add chopped red pepper and continue to sauté for a further 2 minutes

4. Add pasta sauce and allow to come to the boil before switching off the sauté function.

5. Add the penne pasta as well as the water*. Stir to combine.

6. Cook at high pressure for 4 minutes. Allow a natural release for 5 minutes and then quick release.

7. Remove lid and switch to sauté function to reduce sauce a little. Simmer for 5 minutes.

8. Stir in cream and cheese and allow to melt.

Serving Suggestion: Serve with garlic bread and salad.

*How much water you put in will largely depend on how thick your pasta sauce is that you are adding. For thicker sauces add a little more water, and for thinner sauces add a little less. The measurements in this recipe work with the sauce made from this book.

SOUPS

TOMATO AND RED CHILLI SOUP

Serves 4-6

25g butter
1 onion, chopped
2 cloves garlic, crushed
1 red chilli, chopped (remove seeds for a milder taste)
400g tomatoes, chopped
1 large potato, peeled and diced
750ml pint vegetable stock
1 bay leaf
150ml single cream

1. Heat butter in pressure cooker. Add onion and garlic and sauté for 3 to 4 minutes.

2. Add the chilli, tomatoes and potato and gently cook for a further 2 minutes.

3. Switch off the sauté function and add the stock and bay leaf.

4. Cook at high pressure for 5 minutes. Release pressure quickly taking care not to burn yourself.

5. Take the lid off and remove the bay leaf. Blend the soup using a hand blender.

6. Stir in the cream and serve.

Serving Suggestion: Add grated cheese to soup and allow to melt. Serve with crusty bread.

SPICED PARSNIP SOUP

Serves 4-6

1 tbsp olive oil
1 onion, chopped
1 garlic clove, crushed
1 medium potato, peeled and diced
700g parsnips, sliced
1tsp ground coriander
½ tsp ground cumin
½ tsp ground turmeric
½ tsp chilli powder
1 litre chicken or vegetable stock
100ml single cream

1. Heat oil in pot. Add onion and garlic and sauté for 3 to 4 minutes.

2. Switch off sauté function and add remaining ingredients, apart from the cream.

3. Cook at high pressure for 10 minutes

4. Perform a quick release and remove lid.

5. Optional: blend soup using a hand blender or other blender (taking care not to burn yourself)

6. Stir in cream and serve.

CREAM OF MUSHROOM SOUP

Serves 4

1 tbsp olive oil
500g button mushrooms, finely sliced
40g butter
1 small onion, finely sliced
2 garlic cloves, crushed
1 medium potato, peeled and diced
450ml vegetable stock
450ml milk
50ml single cream
Fresh basil leaves to garnish (optional)

1. Heat the oil and butter and sauté the onion, garlic and the mushrooms. Gently sauté for 3 to 4 minutes.

2. Add some of the stock to deglaze the pot if necessary.

3. Switch off the sauté function and add the remaining ingredients apart from the cream and basil.

4. Put the pressure cooker lid on and cook on high pressure for 5 minutes.

5. Perform a quick release and remove the lid.

6. Using a hand blender, blend the soup until smooth.

7. Stir in the single cream.

8. Optional: serve with fresh basil leaves sprinkled on top.

SPLIT PEA SOUP

Serves 4

1 tbsp vegetable oil
4 slices of bacon, chopped
1 onion, chopped
1 litre of vegetable stock
100g split peas
1tsp mixed herbs

1. Heat oil in inner pot

2. Add bacon and onions and sauté for 3 to 4 minutes

3. Switch off sauté and add stock, peas and mixed herbs

4. High pressure for 15 minutes and then quick release

5. Blend if a smooth soup is required

CAULIFLOWER & BUTTERNUT SQUASH SOUP

Serves 4-6

500g butternut squash, diced
2 onions, chopped
4 garlic cloves, crushed
1 tablespoon olive oil
2 tsp paprika
2 bay leaves
1 litre chicken stock
1 head cauliflower, remove and use florets
300ml double cream

1. Heat the oil in your pressure cooker pot. Add the onion and garlic and sauté for 4-5 minutes.

2. Add spices and stir.

3. Add stock and stir to remove any bits stuck to bottom of pot.

4. Add butternut squash to the pot, along with the cauliflower florets.

5. Cook on high pressure for 6 minutes. Allow natural pressure release.

6. Blend using a hand blender. Stir in half the cream. If you prefer a creamier soup, stir in the remaining cream.

SWEET & PEPPERY FRENCH ONION SOUP

Serves 4

1 tbsp olive oil
1 tbsp butter
4 medium onions, thinly sliced
1 tsp salt
¼ tsp pepper
1-inch piece of ginger, thinly sliced
900ml beef stock
200ml sherry
Large chunk of French bread, cubed
Gruyere cheese, shredded, or four slices

1. Add oil and butter to pressure cooker pot and heat until butter is melted.

2. Add onions and stir to coat the slices. Gently cook for 10 minutes, stirring every 3 minutes.

3. Sprinkle onions with salt and pepper and stir. Add ginger to pot, making sure it gets coated with oil.

4. Continue cooking onions for 30 to 35 minutes, stirring approximately every 5 minutes to prevent onions from burning. (If onions are not browning, increase sauté heat.)

5. Add sherry carefully to pot and scrape up any bits of onions that are stuck. Sauté approximately 10 minutes to let most of sherry cook out.

6. Add beef stock to pot. Cook on high pressure 10 minutes, and natural pressure release.

7. While the soup is cooking, cut French bread into cubes and bake at 180 degrees C/gas mark 4 for about 10 minutes in oven until lightly browned and crisp.

8. Once pressure has released, sauté to thicken soup if desired.

9. Spoon into oven-safe bowls, toss in croutons and cover with cheese. Place under a grill for 1-2 minutes to brown.

Tip: This French onion soup is sweet spicy. To make it less sweet, use white wine instead of sherry.

CHICKEN CABBAGE SOUP

Serves 4

½ tbsp. olive oil
4 chicken breasts
250ml water
1 small head cabbage, chopped in large pieces
1 onion, diced
4 carrots, chopped
3 garlic cloves, sliced thin
½ tsp salt
¼ tsp ground ginger
1 litre chicken stock

1. Lightly grease pot with olive oil. Add 1 cup of water to pot and place chicken in water.

2. Cook chicken on high pressure for 10 minutes, natural pressure release for 10 minutes, and then manually release remaining steam.

3. Press cancel to turn the pressure cooker off, and remove chicken to a plate. Shred cooked chicken with utensils.

4. Return the shredded chicken to the pot, along with all other ingredients. Stir to make sure the spices are distributed.

5. Cook on high pressure 5 minutes, natural pressure release 5 minutes, and then release remaining steam.

LENTIL AND POTATO SOUP

Serves 4-6

1 tbsp olive oil
½ onion, sliced
4 garlic cloves, crushed
2 tsp ground cumin
1 tsp salt
¼ tsp pepper
200g green lentils
3 medium potatoes, peeled and cubed
750ml chicken/vegetable stock

1. Heat the oil in your pressure cooker pot on a gentle heat. Sauté the onion until softened, about 5 minutes.

2. Add the garlic and spices to pot, and sauté for 1 minute more. Cancel the sauté function.

3. Add the lentils, potatoes and stock to the pot. Stir well to combine.

4. Cook on high pressure for 12 minutes. Natural pressure release for 10 minutes before slowly releasing remaining pressure.

SPICY PUMPKIN SOUP

Serves 4

800g pumpkin flesh (or 1 x 425g can pumpkin puree)
1 red chilli, finely sliced (remove seeds for a milder taste)
1 tsp salt
1 tsp ground cumin
2 garlic cloves, crushed
1 tsp ground ginger (or 2 tsp fresh)
½ tsp ground cloves
750ml chicken/vegetable stock
60ml double cream

1. Combine all ingredients, except for the cream in the pressure cooker pot. Stir to combine well.

2. Cook on high pressure for 15 minutes, and allow a natural pressure release.

3. Stir in the double cream.

MINESTRONE SOUP

Serves 6

1 tbsp olive oil
½ onion, diced
2 garlic cloves, crushed
½ courgette
2 medium carrots, sliced
2 x 400g tins of chopped tomatoes
200g dry pasta (shells or spirals)
750ml chicken stock
1 tbsp Italian seasoning
1 tsp salt
¼ tsp pepper
30g spinach, chopped
1 x 400g can kidney beans
1 x 400g cannellini beans

1. Heat the oil in the pressure cooker pot. Sauté the onion and garlic in oil until soft, about 5 minutes.

2. Add the courgette, chopped tomatoes, pasta, stock and spices to the pot. Stir to combine.

3. Cook on high pressure for 4 minutes. Allow a natural pressure release for 5 minutes, before manually releasing.

4. Leave on warm and add the spinach and beans to the soup. Heat until all ingredients are warmed through.

Tip: After cooking, the pasta will continue to absorb liquid. Keep extra stock and tomatoes on hand for reheating.

SIDE DISHES & SMALL MEALS

POTATO DAUPHINOIS

Serves 4

400g potatoes, peeled and very thinly sliced
125ml double cream
100g cheddar cheese, grated
25g parmesan cheese, grated
Butter for greasing

You will also need: Lightly greased heatproof dish and trivet.

1. Wash the sliced potatoes in water to wash off any starch. Lightly pat dry.

2. Divide the potato slices up into 3 piles. Layer the first third of potatoes across the base of the dish. Spoon a third of the cream over the potatoes.

3. Mix the cheddar and parmesan cheese together. Sprinkle a third of the cheese over the cream.

4. Repeat this process twice more; potatoes, cream, cheese, until you finish up with a layer of cheese.

5. Cover the dish with baking paper or foil to prevent any moisture dripping in.

6. Pour 375ml (¾ pint) into the pressure cooker pot. Place a trivet inside the pot and lower the dish on top of the trivet. You may want to use a folded tea towel or foil as a makeshift sling as discussed in the introduction.

7. Cook at high pressure for 25 minutes and then reduce pressure quickly (quick release).

8. Carefully take the dish from the pressure cooker and remove the paper/foil.

9. For a delicious finish brown the cheese off by placing the whole dish under a grill for a few minutes.

Serving Suggestion: Eat as a starter or as a side to a meat or fish dish.

RATATOUILLE

Serves 4

2tbsp olive oil
1tsp dried marjoram
1tsp Herbes de Provence
1 onion, chopped
2 cloves garlic, crushed
1 aubergine, diced
1 red pepper, deseeded and sliced
1 green pepper, deseeded and sliced
200g tomatoes, chopped
200g courgettes, chopped
250ml water

1. Heat the oil. Add the onion and garlic and gently sauté for 4 to 5 minutes.

2. Add the aubergine and peppers and continue to sauté for a further 2 to 3 minutes.

3. Switch off the sauté function and add the remaining ingredients. Gently stir to combine.

4. After placing the lid on the pressure cooker, cook on high pressure for 3 minutes.

5. Reduce the pressure quickly with a quick release.

Serving Suggestion: Serve as a side with chicken, or on its own as a starter.

BRUSSEL SPROUTS & PANCETTA

Serves 4-6

2 tbsp olive oil
1 red onion, sliced
3 cloves garlic, crushed
100g pancetta
500g brussel sprouts
100ml vegetable stock
1tbsp Dijon mustard
1tsp ground nutmeg

1. Heat the oil in the pressure cooker and add the onion and garlic. Gently sauté for 5 minutes.

2. Add the pancetta and cook for a further 3 minutes.

3. Add the brussel sprouts, nutmeg and mustard and gently sauté for 1 minute.

4. Switch off the sauté function and add the vegetable stock.

5. Set to high pressure for 3 minutes and then release quickly (quick release.)

Serving Suggestion: serve as a started or as a side for a main meal.

BAKED BEANS

4 to 6 servings

400g tin cannellini beans, drained
1 tbsp vegetable oil
1 onion, chopped
1 tsp mustard powder
1 tsp Worcestershire sauce
2 tbsp tomato puree
150ml passata
1 tbsp soft brown sugar
300ml vegetable stock
Pinch Allspice
Salt and pepper to season

1. Heat oil and sauté onions for 5 minutes

2. Switch off sauté and add remaining ingredients. Stir together

3. Put lid on and set to high pressure for 30 minutes

4. Quick release

5. Simmer for 10 to 15 minutes on sauté setting to allow sauce to thicken up. If a runnier consistency is preferred simmer for less time or add some more stock.

Serving Suggestion: Tastes great on toast, or poured over a baked potato.

THAI FRAGRANT RICE

Serves 4

1 piece lemongrass
2 limes
200g long grain rice, rinsed
1 tbsp olive oil
1 onion, chopped
2.5cm/1 inch fresh root ginger
1 ½ tsp coriander seeds
1 ½ tsp cumin seeds
600ml vegetable stock

1. Chop lemongrass finely and remove the zest from the limes. Remove the juice from the limes as set to one side.

2. Heat oil. Add onions, spices, ginger, lime zest and lemongrass and cook for 2 to 3 minutes.

3. Add rice and cook for 1 minute.

4. Add stock and juice from limes. Cook on high pressure for 4 minutes. Allow to natural release for 5 minutes before releasing manually (quick release).

5. Remove lid and fluff up with a fork.

SPICY THAI OMELETTE

Serves 4

1tbsp olive oil
4 medium eggs
3 spring onions, finely sliced
1 tomato, finely sliced
½ tsp fish sauce
½ red pepper, finely sliced
½ red chilli, finely sliced
1 clove garlic, crushed
50g pork or turkey mince

You Will Also Need: Heatproof casserole dish and trivet

1. In a mixing bowl, whisk together the eggs. Add the spring onions, tomato, chilli, pepper and fish sauce.

2. In the pressure cooker heat the oil and gently sauté the pork or turkey mince with the crushed garlic. Cook for a few minutes until the mince has browned.

3. Remove the meat mixture from the pressure cooker pot and transfer to the casserole dish. Wash out the pressure cooker pot.

4. Pour the egg mixture in with the meat and mix together.

5. Pour 1 cup of water into the pressure cooker. Place the trivet in the pot and lower the casserole dish on top. Cover the dish with a lid, baking paper or foil. You may want to use a folded tea towel or foil as a makeshift sling as discussed in the introduction.

6. Cook at high pressure for 10 minutes and release quickly (quick release).

7. Carefully lift the dish out of the pressure cooker and turn upside down to remove omelette.

Serving Suggestion: Serve as a light lunch or part of a main meal.

EGG FRIED RICE

Serves 4

1tbsp vegetable oil
1 medium onion, chopped
2 cloves garlic, crushed
1 medium egg
200g basmati rice, rinsed
2tbsp soy sauce
250ml cup vegetable stock
100g frozen peas

1. Heat the oil in the pressure cooker pot. Add the onion, garlic and rice and gently sauté for 2 to 3 minutes.

2. Add the egg and cook it until it resembles scrambled egg.

3. Switch off the sauté function and add the soy sauce and vegetable stock.

4. Put the lid on and cook at high pressure for 6 minutes. Release the pressure quickly (quick release) and remove the lid.

5. Stir in the frozen peas, gently mixing for a few minutes.

LEMON & CHILLI RICE

400g basmati rice, rinsed
Equal part water (1 pint)
1 tbsp olive oil
1 small onion, finely chopped
1 small red chilli, sliced
1tsp grated fresh root ginger
1tsp ground turmeric
1tsp ground cayenne pepper
Juice of 1 lemon

1. Heat oil in pressure cooker pot. Sauté onion, chilli and ginger.

2. Add spices, sauté for further 30 seconds.

3. Add rice and gently sauté for 30 seconds.

4. Switch off, add water and stir to combine.

5. Place the lid on and cook at high pressure for 6 minutes. Allow natural release for 5 minutes and then manually release.

6. Remove lid and fluff up with a fork.

JAMAICAN RICE & PEAS

Serves 4

2 tbsp olive oil
1 onion, chopped
1 red pepper, deseeded and chopped
400g long grain rice, rinsed
400ml coconut milk
400ml water
½ tsp dried thyme
200g tin red kidney beans

1. Heat oil in pressure cooker pot. Add onion and sauté for 2 minutes.

2. Add red pepper and sauté for a further 1 to 2 minutes.

3. Add rice and sauté for 1 minute.

4. Add remaining ingredients and mix.

5. High pressure for 6 minutes and natural release for 5 minutes.

SPICY STUFFED GREEN PEPPER STEW

Serves 4

500g minced beef
½ medium onion, sliced
2 garlic cloves, crushed
2 large green peppers, chopped
1 x 400g can chopped tomatoes
1 x 400g passata
125ml beef stock
90g brown basmati rice, uncooked
½ tsp salt
¼ tsp pepper

1. Heat oil in pressure cooker pot. Add the minced beef, onion and garlic until the beef is fully browned.

2. Add the remaining ingredients. Stir to mix.

3. Cook on high pressure for 15 minutes, and natural release for 10 minutes, before releasing remaining steam.

SOUTHWEST POTATOES

Serves 4

12 new potatoes, halved lengthwise
1 tbsp olive oil
½ tsp cayenne
1 tsp garlic powder
1 tsp cumin
½ tsp salt
½ tsp pepper
60ml vegetable stock
1 x 400g can chopped tomatoes (liquid drained out)

You Will Also Need: Trivet or steamer basket

1. Add oil to pot and heat to spread over surface. Add potatoes and sauté until lightly browned.

2. Sprinkle half of each spice over the potatoes as they cook. Once browned, remove the potatoes from the pot.

3. Pour in the stock, scrape the bottom to lift up any browned bits.

4. Add in any tomatoes, add the rest of the spices and stir.

5. Put the potatoes in a steamer basket, or layer on a trivet over the stock and tomatoes.

6. Cook on high pressure for 5 minutes then natural pressure release for 5 minutes, before quick releasing.

Serving Suggestion: Top with sprinkled cheese or sour cream.

COCONUT RICE

Serves 2-4

180g white rice
1 tbsp coconut oil
250ml coconut milk
125ml water
¼ tsp salt
¼ tsp cinnamon
¼ tsp ginger

1. Rinse rice in cold water.

2. Add the coconut oil to the pressure cooker pot. Put on warm and stir around until pot is coated.

3. Stir the rice. Add round ⅔ of the coconut milk, water, and all spices into the pot.

4. High pressure for 4 minutes and allow pressure to release naturally.

5. When finished, stir in the rest of the coconut milk.

Tip: Try with mango cherry salsa.

STEAMED VEGETABLE DUMPLINGS

Serves 8-10

320g flour
¼ tsp salt
150ml boiling water
5 tbsp cold water
50g cabbage, finely chopped
5g chives, finely chopped
15g carrot, grated
20g mushrooms, chopped
1 tsp ginger, minced
1 tbsp soy sauce

1. Mix flour and salt in a bowl. Add hot water and stir in until mixture resembles breadcrumbs.

2. Add cold water and stir rapidly to mix. Knead in bowl to pick up all flour.

3. Place on a counter and knead 5-7 minutes until dough is a firm ball.

4. Return to the bowl and cover with a damp towel. Allow to stand for 20 minutes.

5. Whilst the dough stands, salt the cabbage and leave to sit.

6. Separate the dough into 40 small balls. Flatten each ball in hand and roll out until you can see the surface beneath the dough, making it thinner at edges.

7. Squeeze the water out of the cabbage. Place in a bowl with the other vegetables and soy sauce. Mix well. Add roughly 1 teaspoon of mixture to each dumpling. Pinch edges together, making sure dough seals completely.

8. Place the dumplings in a steamer basket in a single layer. Add 1 cup of water to the pot along with the steamer basket. Cook on high pressure for 7 minutes and allow to natural pressure release for 5 minutes, then manual release.

ROOT VEGETABLES IN SPINACH-ARTICHOKE SAUCE

Serves 4

1 tbsp olive oil
4 cloves garlic, finely sliced
125ml chicken stock
300g tin artichoke hearts, chopped
150g fresh baby spinach, stems removed and ripped in half
Pinch salt
Pinch pepper
8 new potatoes
8 radishes
8 medium carrots
225g cream cheese
100g mozzarella cheese, grated
2 tbsp grated parmesan cheese

1. Heat oil in pressure cooker pot. Sauté the garlic until soft (about 3 minutes).

2. Add the chicken stock, artichokes, spinach, salt and pepper to the pot and stir.

3. Place the vegetables in a steamer basket and place in the pot. Place the trivet in the stock mixture and layer vegetables on top.

4. Cook on high pressure for 5 minutes and then quick release pressure.

5. Remove the steamer basket with the vegetables, or vegetable and trivet, from the pot. Leave the mixture on warm.

6. Stir in the cream cheese and parmesan until fully melted and warm.

7. Pour mixture over vegetables.

MEXICAN BLACK BEANS

Serves 4

1 x 400g can black beans
175g frozen sweet corn
190g brown rice
350ml water
200g salsa
¼ tsp chilli powder
½ tsp garlic powder
1 tsp cumin
¼ tsp salt

1. Add all the ingredients to the pot, and stir to mix well.

2. Cook on high pressure for 18 minutes, and then natural pressure release.

SWEET POTATO MASH

Serves 4

500g sweet potatoes, peeled and cubed
500g white potatoes, peeled and cubed
2 tbsp coconut oil
125ml chicken stock
30ml double cream
50ml milk to desired fluffiness

1. Melt the coconut oil in the pressure cooker pot on keep warm to coat pan.

2. Add the stock to the pot and place the trivet or steamer basket inside. Layer potatoes on the trivet, or in the basket.

3. Cook on high pressure for 10 minutes and then natural pressure release. Remove inner pot to heat-resistant surface.

4. Remove the trivet or basket from the pot, placing the potatoes into the stock. Mash the potatoes with the potato masher.

5. Stir in the cream and milk until smooth.

SPICY COCONUT CREAMED CORN

Serves 4

2 tbsp salted butter
300g frozen sweet corn
250ml chicken/vegetable stock
1 inch piece of ginger
Pinch of ground black pepper
Pinch of ground cayenne pepper
80ml coconut milk

1. Heat butter on warm in pot until melted.

2. Add all the ingredients, except the coconut milk, to the pot and stir.

3. Cook on high pressure for 10 minutes and then natural pressure release.

4. Remove the ginger from the pot, and throw away.

5. Sauté on high until stock evaporates (approximately 10 minutes).

6. Remove from the heat and stir in coconut milk.

Tip: Coconut milk separates whilst stored. Make sure it is well mixed before adding to recipe.

GARLIC GREEN BEANS

Serves 4

300g fresh green beans, ends removed
1 tbsp olive oil
1 tsp salt
¼ tsp pepper
2 garlic cloves, crushed

1. Add 1 cup of water to pot.

2. Put the oil, salt and pepper into a clear plastic sandwich bag. Put the green beans in, a few at a time, tossing the bag to coat with oil.

3. Layer the green beans in a steamer basket.

4. Sprinkle minced garlic cloves over the beans.

5. Cook high pressure 0 minutes, and quick pressure release.

SPICY COUSCOUS

Serves 4

1 tbsp fresh root ginger, grated
1 large onion, chopped
1 tbsp olive oil
1 large carrot, grated
1 large tomato, chopped
1 red pepper, deseeded and chopped
1 tsp ground cumin
1 tsp ground cinnamon
1 tsp ground coriander
1 tbsp tomato puree
50g raisins
400ml water
200g couscous
1 tbsp freshly squeezed lemon juice
Salt and pepper to season

1. Heat oil in inner pot. Add onion and sauté for 2 to 3 minutes.

2. Add carrot, pepper, tomato, ginger and spices. Sauté for a further minute, stirring.

3. Add water, couscous, raisins and tomato puree.

4. Cook on high pressure for 2 minutes and then allow to natural release for 10 minutes before quick releasing.

5. Stir through lemon juice.

BREAKFASTS

EGG, HAM & CHEESE FRITTATA

Serves 4

4 medium eggs
1 tbsp milk
80g grated cheddar cheese
80g cooked, chopped bacon/sliced ham

You Will Also Need: 4 ramekin dishes and trivet

1. Whisk together the eggs and milk.

2. Pour the mixture evenly between the 4 ramekin dishes

3. Add some bacon/ham and grated cheese between each dish.

4. Pour 1 cup of water into the pressure cooker. Place the trivet in the pot and lower each ramekin dish on top.

5. Cook at high pressure for 5 minutes and then release quickly (quick release).

Serving Suggestion: to add a little green to your breakfast, add some chopped up baby spinach leaves to the mix.

FRUIT QUINOA BREAKFAST

Serves 4

175g quinoa
375ml almond milk
10 dried apricots, chopped
40g raisins
1 tsp vanilla extract

1. Thoroughly rinse quinoa

2. Add all ingredients and gently mix together

3. High pressure for 1 minute

4. Natural release

BANANA MAPLE BUCKWHEAT

Serves 4

½ tbsp coconut oil
2 large bananas, mashed into a smooth puree
600ml water
1 tbsp butter
320g maple syrup
160g buckwheat
¼ tsp allspice

1. Turn unit on warm and add coconut oil to pot. Spread oil over pot.

2. Add pureed bananas, water, butter and maple syrup. Stir as it warms until butter melts and maple syrup dissolves.

3. Add the buckwheat and allspice, and whisk to remove lumps.

4. Cook at high pressure for 3 minutes. Allow pressure to release naturally.

5. Whisk again before serving.

OLIVE & GOAT CHEESE FRITTATA

Serves 4

4 medium eggs
2 tbsp double cream
12 black olives, sliced
2 tbsp goat cheese, crumbled
Pinch ground black pepper
Pinch paprika

You Will Also Need: 4 ramekin dishes

1. Whisk the eggs and cream in bowl.

2. Add the olives, goat cheese and spices. Stir to mix.

3. Pour into four 7 ounce ramekins

4. Cook on high pressure for 5 minutes, and quick release.

Tip: Black olives and goat cheese make for a very flavourful frittata. Skip the salt and go easy on the spices.

RICE AND OAT PORRIDGE

Serves 4

1 tbsp coconut oil
700ml water
1 ½ tbsp vanilla extract
1 ½ tbsp almond extract
80g honey
80g maple syrup
90g rolled oats
185g white rice

1. Put on warm and add coconut oil to pot. Spread around to coat.

2. Add water, extracts, honey and maple syrup to pot, and stir until honey and maple syrup are dissolved.

3. Whisk in oats and rice.

4. Cook on high pressure for 10 minutes, and then natural pressure release.

CHUTNEYS & JAMS

There is no end to the variety of jams, preserves and chutneys you can create in your pressure cooker. One of the many benefits the pressure cooker brings is shortened cooking times. Softening fruit for jams and marmalades can be a lengthy process when done via the traditional method; using a pressure cooker shortens the time considerably.

Storage

Any jams, chutneys or preserves that you intend to store or give as gifts need to be stored in clean, sterilised jars, and then kept in a cool, dry place.

Sterilising Jars

Jars can be sterilised by one of the following methods;

- Run through a complete dishwasher cycle.
- Washed with hot soapy water, rinsed and then placed in a microwave for 1 minute on high.
- Washed with hot soapy water, rinsed and place in an oven on a low temperature for 30 minutes.

APRICOT JAM

Makes approx 3 standard sized jam jars (1lb/370ml)

500g dried apricots
1 litre boiling water
Juice of 2 lemons
1kg caster sugar

1. Place dried apricots in pressure cooker pot. Cover with the boiling water. Put the lid on the pressure cooker (without switching anything on), and leave them for about an hour.

2. Add the lemon juice and cook on low pressure for 10 minutes. Allow pressure to release naturally.

3. Remove the lid and mash the apricots down into a liquid.

4. Switch the sauté function on to the lowest heat. Add the sugar and stir over a low heat until completely dissolved.

5. Switch the sauté function up to the highest temperature and allow the jam to boil vigorously until the setting point* has been achieved. This normally takes anywhere between 5 and 20 minutes. As the mixture boils you will need to skim the surface with a ladle to remove any layers that form.

6. Spoon into hot and sterilised jam jars, leaving a little room at the top before sealing the container with the lids.

*Setting Point Test

Spoon out a little of the mix and leave it on a cold plate to cool. When it has cooled down it should have a gel like consistency when you touch it. Alternatively if you have a sugar/candy thermometer wait until the temperature reaches 104C/220F.

ORANGE MARMALADE

Makes: approx 1.5kg/3lb

500g Seville oranges (or any sweet orange if Seville are out of season)
1 pint water
2 tbsp lemon juice
1kg sugar

You will also need: Muslin bag and sterilised jam jars

1. Wash the fruit by scrubbing it. Cut both the oranges and lemons into quarters and squeeze out the juice into the pressure cooker pot. Remove the pips and scrape out as much of the pulp as you can, placing both the pips and pulp in a muslin bag. Tie the muslin bag loosely at the top.

2. Slice the orange skins thinly, or shred them, depending on your preferences. Add them to the juice in the pressure cooker pot, together with half the water, and the muslin bag of pips and pulp.

3. Cook on high pressure for 10 minutes. Allow the pressure to release naturally.

4. Remove the lid and remove the bag. Squeeze as much of the juice from the bag as possible, back into the pressure cooker pot.

5. Switch the sauté function on low and add the remaining water and the sugar to the pressure cooker pot (optional: warm the sugar before adding to help it dissolve more easily).

6. Once the sugar has completely dissolved turn the heat up until the mixture is boiling rapidly. Cook until setting point* has been reached. This normally takes anywhere between 5 and 20 minutes but can take longer**. As the mixture boils you will need to skim the surface with a ladle to remove any layers that form.

7. Optional: If you prefer a shredless marmalade (marmalade without the skin) you can use a metal sieve at this point to make it smooth.

8. Spoon into hot and sterilised jam jars, leaving a little room at the top before sealing the container with the lids.

*Setting Point Test

Spoon out a little of the mix and leave it on a cold plate to cool. When it has cooled down it should have a gel like consistency when you touch it. Alternatively if you have a sugar/candy thermometer wait until the temperature reaches 104C/220F.

** If the mixture just doesn't seem to be setting you may need to boil it for longer. I have had some batches that haven't set within this time and so I have just continued boiling it. Be careful not to over boil it though or you'll end up with a dark toffee like syrup!

MINCEMEAT

500g Granny Smiths or cooking apples, peeled, cored and diced into tiny cubes
200g soft brown sugar
150g sultanas
150g raisins
150g currants
50g glace cherries, chopped
150g vegetarian suet, grated
100g mixed peel, chopped
300ml apple juice
Zest and juice of 1 lemons
Zest and juice of 1 orange
$\frac{1}{2}$ tsp ground ginger
1tsp mixed spice
1tsp ground cinnamon
1tsp ground nutmeg
$\frac{1}{4}$ tsp ground cloves
150ml brandy/rum (optional)
60g almonds, chopped (optional)

You Will Also Need: Sterilised jam jars to store

1. Combine all the ingredients in the pressure cooker pot apart from the brandy/rum and the almonds. Stir well to make sure all the ingredients are mixed together.

2. Cook on low pressure for 10 minutes and allow a natural release.

3. If you are adding brandy/rum and/or almonds, add now and stir in.

4. Switch the pressure cooker to the sauté mode and gently simmer the mixture for 5 to 10 minutes, or until the desired consistency is reached.

Want To Make Mince Pies?

Mince pies are the perfect Christmas treat, especially with a bit of added ice cream or brandy butter. Simply make some pastry (simple pastry recipe below) or buy some readymade. Preheat oven to 350F/180C/Gas Mark 4 and grease a cake/tartlet tray. Roll out pastry to a thickness of about 1cm/½ inch. Use round cutters to cut out circles of approximately 7cm/2½ inches. Lay circles into cake tray and half fill each pie with the above mincemeat. Cut out either star shapes, or slightly smaller circles to use as lids for the pies. Glaze the surface of each pie with a little milk. Cook in the oven for about 15 minutes, or until golden in colour. Sprinkle with icing sugar before serving.

Pastry

200g/7oz plain flour, plus extra for rolling.
100g/3 ½ oz butter
25g/1oz icing sugar + a little for sprinkling
1 egg yolk
3 tbsp milk + a little for glazing

1. Sift the flour into a mixing bowl. Add the butter and rub into the flour with your fingertips until the mixture has a breadcrumb like texture.

2. Add the sugar, egg yolk and milk. Mix together to make a soft dough.

3. Lightly flour a work surface and gently knead the dough until smooth. Roll out dough and fill with mincemeat as per the instructions above.

SPICED APPLE CHUTNEY

750g cooking apples, peeled, cored and chopped into small cubes
2 garlic cloves, crushed
½ tsp cayenne pepper
1 tsp mixed spice
½ tsp salt
200ml malt vinegar
30g stem or crystallised ginger, chopped
150g soft brown sugar
100g sultanas (or other mixed dried fruits)

1. Place all the ingredients in the pressure cooker pot and stir well.

2. Set pressure cooker to high pressure for 8 minutes.

3. Allow natural release for 10 minutes and then quick release.

4. Gently sauté the mixture until it has a thick consistency, stirring continuously.

5. Spoon into sterilised jars.

Chutney will last for 6 months unopened and stored in a dark place. Once opened, store in a fridge and use within 4 weeks.

LEMON CURD

3 medium eggs
200g (8oz) caster sugar
Zest of 2 lemons
3tbsp lemon juice
50g (2oz) unsalted butter

You Will Also Need: heatproof dish and trivet

1. Beat eggs and pour into heatproof dish.

2. Add the lemon zest, juice and sugar. Stir well.

3. Chop the butter up into small cubes/chunks and dot over the top.

4. Cover the dish with baking paper or foil.

5. Add 250ml (½ pint) of water, plus a squirt of lemon juice, to the pressure cooker pot and place the trivet inside. Lower the heatproof dish on top of the trivet.

6. Cook on high pressure for 10 minutes. Allow a natural release.

7. Remove the dish from the pressure cooker and stir the lemon curd well.

8. Transfer to a sterilised jar.

Serving Suggestion: Tastes great on pancakes, or as part of a lemon sponge cake.

CHAI PEACH PRESERVES

Serves 4

450g frozen peaches
½ tbsp honey
½ tbsp sugar
Juice of half a lemon
Pinch ground cinnamon
Pinch ground ginger
Pinch ground cardamom
Pinch ground cloves

1. Add the honey and sugar to the pot. Stir on warm until sugar melts and honey dissolves.

2. Add all the other ingredients to the pot. Stir to mix.

3. Cook on high pressure for 3 minutes, and let naturally pressure release.

4. Sauté to reduce water by half.

5. Mash with potato masher or fork to crush big pieces.

DESSERTS & SWEET TREATS

SPICED FRUIT LOAF

200g self raising flour
Pinch of baking powder
Pinch of salt
75g margarine
100g raisins or sultanas or dried mixed fruit
50g sugar
1tsp ground nutmeg
1 medium egg, beaten
1tbsp milk

You Will Also Need: Lightly greased loaf tin and trivet

1. Sieve the flour, baking powder and salt into a mixing bowl. Add the margarine and mix together with your fingertips until a breadcrumb like consistency is achieved.

2. Add the sugar, fruit and nutmeg. Pour in the beaten egg and milk. Mix together until a dough has formed. Add a little more milk if needed.

3. Transfer the dough into the loaf tin and pat down, smoothing the top.

4. Cover with baking paper or foil to prevent any moisture dripping in.

5. Pour 750ml boiling water into the pressure cooker pot and place the trivet inside. Place the baking tin on the trivet. You may want to use a folded tea towel or foil as a makeshift sling as discussed in the introduction.

6. Set to low pressure for 45 minutes and allow a natural release.

7. Optional: Brown off under a hot grill.

Serving Suggestion: Tastes great with a spread of warm jam or syrup on top.

BLUEBERRY & APPLE COBBLER

Filling
400g blueberries
2 dessert apples, peeled, cored and thinly sliced
1 tbsp caster sugar + some to sprinkle
Finely grated zest of ½ lemon

Cobbler
225g self-raising flour
2tsp baking powder
75g caster sugar
Pinch of salt
75g unsalted butter
100ml buttermilk
1 medium egg

You will also need: heatproof dish and a trivet.

1. Add the blueberries and apples to your heatproof dish and mix in the sugar and lemon zest.

2. In a separate mixing bowl, sift the flour, baking powder, caster sugar and salt. Add the butter and mix all the ingredients together with your fingertips until you get a breadcrumb like consistency.

3. In another mixing bowl, combine the buttermilk and egg. Add the beaten mixture to the breadcrumb mixture and combine until a dough has been formed.

4. Separate the dough into approximately 6 ball shapes and arrange them on top of the fruit, allowing space between them. Sprinkle a little caster sugar over the top. Cover the dish with foil or baking paper to prevent any moisture dripping into the cake.

5. Pour 2 cups of water into the pressure cooker pot. Place a trivet inside the pot and lower the dish on top of the trivet. You may want to use a folded tea towel or foil as a makeshift sling as discussed in the introduction.

6. Cook at high pressure for 10 minutes. Allow pressure to release naturally.

GERMAN APPLE CAKE

175g unsalted butter, softened
175g light soft brown sugar
3 medium eggs, beaten
175g self raising flour
3tbsp milk
2 dessert apples
Topping:
115g plain flour
85g light soft brown sugar
2tsp ground cinnamon
85g unsalted butter

You Will Also Need: 20cm/8inch baking tin and a trivet.

To make the topping:

1. In a mixing bowl, combine the flour, sugar and cinnamon together.

2. Add the butter, rubbing it in gently with your fingers until a crumbly dough is formed.

3. Wrap the dough in cling film and allow to chill in the refrigerator for half an hour.

4. Lightly grease a 20cm (8inch) baking tin.

5. In a bowl, whisk together butter and sugar until smooth.

6. Mix in the lemon zest.

7. Gradually add the beaten eggs, stirring as you add them.

8. Sift the flour into the mixture and gently mix together.

9. Add the milk and gently mix a little more.

10. Take half of the mixture and spread it in the greased baking tin. Smooth it out using a knife.

11. Take half of the apple slices and arrange over the top of the batter.

12. Spread the remaining mixture over the apples and smooth over.

13. Place the remaining apple slices on the batter.

14. Take the chilled dough from the refrigerator and grate it. Sprinkle the grated dough over the top of the cake in the tin. Cover the cake tin with foil or baking paper to prevent any moisture dripping into the cake.

15. Pour 2 cups of water into the pressure cooker pot. Place a trivet inside the pot and lower the baking tin on top of the trivet. You may want to use a folded tea towel or foil as a makeshift sling as discussed in the introduction.

16. Cook at high pressure for 20 minutes. When finished, allow a natural release.

17. Lift the baking tin out of the pressure cooker using the sling and remove the baking paper/foil, taking care not to let any water drip on the cake.

18. Leave the cake to cool slightly before removing it from the tin.

Serving Suggestion: Tastes great with vanilla ice cream or custard.

VANILLA CHEESECAKE

40g unsalted butter, plus extra for greasing
225g Digestive biscuits
1 tbsp light brown soft sugar
600g cream cheese
3 eggs, separated
100 + 30g caster sugar
1tsp vanilla extract
300ml sour cream

You Will Also Need: 8 inch spring form or loose base circular tin and trivet

1. In a large mixing bowl, whisk together the cream cheese, 100g sugar, vanilla extract, and egg yolks.

2. In a separate bowl whisk the eggs whites until stiff, and once completed fold into the cream cheese mixture.

3. Using the method that you find easiest, smash up the digestive biscuits until they are very fine crumbs, but not a powder. I find it easiest to put the biscuits in a food bag and repeatedly strike them with a rolling pin.

4. In another bowl, melt the butter in the microwave (or in a saucepan) and add the biscuit crumbs and light brown soft sugar and mix until well combined. It shouldn't be too wet nor too dry- if it is too wet, add another biscuit, and if it is too dry, add a bit more melted butter.

5. Pour the biscuit mixture into the tin and smooth over with a spoon.

6. Pour the cream cheese mixture on top and smooth over, using a spatula to get out all the cheesy goodness!

7. Place the trivet in the pot and add 300ml water. Cover the tin with foil and using a sling made from foil, or a folded tea towel, lower the tin down onto the trivet.

8. Cook on high pressure for 40 minutes and allow a natural release to prevent the cheesecake from cracking.

9. Carefully remove the cheesecake from the pot and remove the foil cover. Gently remove any water that may be resting on top of the cheesecake by tilting the cake slightly or dabbing it with a paper towel.

10. Mix the sour cream with the 30g caster sugar and pour over the top of the cheesecake and leave to cool.

11. Place cheesecake in the fridge for at least 12 hours to allow it to set.

GOLDEN SYRUP DUMPLINGS

Makes 12

For the dumplings
225g self-raising flour
50g unsalted butter
1 egg
100ml milk

For the syrup
100ml golden syrup
400ml water
100g soft brown sugar
50g butter

1. In a bowl combine 50g of butter with the flour to form breadcrumbs

2. In a separate jug beat the egg. Add the milk and 1 tbsp golden syrup. Whisk together.

3. Add milk and egg mixture into the flour to form a sticky dough.

4. Split the dough to form 12 round dumplings.

5. Switch on the sauté function on your pressure cooker. Melt the butter in the pot and add the sugar, golden syrup and water. Continue to cook until the sugar is completely dissolved.

6. Cancel the sauté function and set the pressure cooker to low pressure for 5 minutes. Release pressure quickly (quick release).

Serving Suggestion: Serve with vanilla ice cream

WHITE CHOCOLATE BROWNIES

75g butter
200g white chocolate chips
3 large eggs
175g golden caster sugar
175g self raising flour
1tsp vanilla extract

You Will Also Need: Lightly greased baking tin + trivet

1. Melt the butter.

2. Whisk the sugar, butter, egg and vanilla extract together.

3. In a separate mixing bowl, sift the flour and salt. Pour the whisked mixture in, continuously stirring.

4. Add the chocolate chips, gently combining in.

5. Transfer mixture into greased baking tin. Cover tin with baking paper or foil.

6. Pour 2 cups of water into the pressure cooker pot. Place the trivet inside and lower the baking tin in. You may want to use a folded tea towel or foil as a makeshift sling as discussed in the introduction.

7. Cook on high pressure for 25 minutes and then allow to release naturally for 10 minutes before manually releasing.

8. Allow the cake to rest for 10 minutes before removing from tin.

EASY PEACH MELBA

Serves 4 - 6

80ml water
50g sugar
Juice of 1 lemon
300g frozen raspberries
300g peaches

1. Add water and sugar to pressure cooker pot. Sauté on lowest heat, stirring until sugar dissolves.

2. Add lemon juice and fruit to the pot.

3. Cook on high pressure for 4 minutes, and then quick pressure release.

4. Remove the peaches from the pot with the slotted spoon, and then place in a bowl with a lid.

5. Sauté and stir whilst cooking until the juice cooks down and thickens until it starts to stick to the spoon.

6. Pour sauce into the bowl with the peaches and chill in refrigerator for 2 hours.

Serving Suggestion: serve over ice cream.

SWEET MAPLE AND PEAR BUTTERNUT SQUASH

Serves 2-4

1 butternut squash
1 pear
4 tbsp maple syrup
1 tbsp butter
1 tbsp pecans, broken into small pieces
¼ tsp ground cinnamon

1. Cut butternut squash vertically and remove seeds and pulp until inside is smooth

2. Peel pear and cut into small pieces. Put ½ into each squash.

3. Pour 2 tbsp maple syrup over each pear and place ½ tbsp butter on each pear in each squash.

4. Add 1 cup water to inner pot, and place butternut squash halves side by side or stacked on a trivet.

5. Pressure cook on high for 6 minutes, and quick pressure release.

6. Remove squash from pot. Sprinkle ½ tbsp pecan pieces and half of cinnamon over each side.

Tip: Squash is difficult cut. To ease the process, precook squash for 3 minutes in pressure cooker, cut after cooking, and then reduce cooking time to 4 minutes in recipe.

PUMPKIN RICE PUDDING

Serves 4

225g pumpkin puree
185g brown rice
350ml water
½ tbsp vanilla extract
1 tbsp butter
¼ tsp cinnamon
¼ tsp ginger
¼ tsp allspice
¼ tsp cardamom
Pinch ground cloves
3 tbsp maple syrup
150g raisins
120ml double cream

1. Add rice, water, vanilla, butter and spices to pressure cooker pot. Stir well.

2. Pressure cook on high for 20 minutes, and natural pressure release.

3. Stir in pumpkin puree, raisins, maple syrup, and cream.

4. Sauté low until warmed through, and remove from heat promptly.

DATE APPLE CRANBERRY SAUCE

Serves 4

2 apples, peeled and cored, chopped small
300g cranberries
240ml cranberry juice
80ml water
85g date syrup (see tip below)
2 tbsp sugar

1. Add cranberry juice, water, syrup and sugar to pot. Stir on warm until syrup is dissolved.

2. Add cranberries. Cook on high pressure for 6 minute. Natural pressure release.

3. Add apples. Press sauté, and sauté until most liquid has evaporated and apples are soft.

Tip: Date syrup isn't always easily available. Some supermarkets stock it and most health food stores do. You can substitute it with maple syrup or better still, try making your own date syrup. It's a great natural sweetener!

Date Syrup
8 dates
300ml water (filtered if possible), plus extra for soaking
1tsp lemon juice

Place the dates in a bowl and cover with boiling water. Cover bowl and allow to sit for 45 minutes. When the time is up, drain the water away and add the dates together with the 300ml water and lemon juice to a high speed blender. Blend for 60 seconds or until smooth. Will keep in the fridge in an airtight container for up to 3 weeks.

SWEET CHOCOLATE DUMPLINGS

Serves 8-10

320ml flour
160ml boiling water
5 tbsp cold water
170g + 1 tsp honey
100g cocoa powder

You Will Also Need: Steamer Basket

1. Add flour to bowl. Add hot water and stir in until mixture resembles breadcrumbs.

2. Add cold water and 1 tsp honey. Stir rapidly to mix. Knead in bowl to pick up all flour.

3. Place on a worktop counter and knead for 5-7 minutes until dough is a firm ball.

4. Return to the bowl and cover with a damp towel. Let stand for 20 minutes.

5. Whilst the dough stands, mix honey and cocoa until fully blended.

6. Separate the dough into 40 small balls. Flatten each ball in hand and roll out until you can see the surface beneath the dough, making it thinner at the edges.

7. Spoon a small amount of chocolate honey into each dumpling. Pinch edges together, making sure dough seals completely.

8. Place dumplings in steamer basket in single layer. Add 1 cup of water to pot along with the steamer basket. Cook on high pressure for 7 minutes, natural pressure release 5 minutes, and then manual release.

EASY CINNAMON APPLES

Serves 4

1 tbsp unsalted butter
1 tbsp honey or maple syrup
2 tbsp water
4 apples, quartered, core and seeds removed
4 dried dates, chopped (or about 40g raisins)
¼ tsp ginger
Pinch ground cardamom

1. Melt butter and honey/maple syrup in water over a warm heat in your pressure cooker.

2. Add all the remaining ingredients and stir around to coat apples and dates in syrup.

3. Cook on high pressure for 1 minute, and then quick release.

Serving suggestion: Top with roasted pecans or other nut.

MAPLE ALMOND CUSTARD

Serves 4

2 medium eggs
4 tbsp maple syrup
330ml milk
Pinch of salt
½ tsp almond extract

You Will Also Need: 4 ramekin dishes

1. Crack eggs into bowl and beat until smooth.

2. Add remaining ingredients and whip until smooth. Pour into 4 7-ounce ramekins.

3. Cook on high pressure for 7 minutes, and natural pressure release.

4. Refrigerate for at least 2 hours.

GINGER VANILLA TEA

Serves 6

1 tbsp honey (or more to taste)

1 inch piece of ginger, cut in six pieces

½ tbsp vanilla extract

6 tea bags

Water

1. Add water to ⅔ full in your pressure cooker pot. Add the honey. Put pot on warm and stir until honey dissolves into water.

2. Add ginger and vanilla to pot. Stir.

3. Add tea bags and cook on high pressure for 8 minutes. Allow pressure to release naturally.

Tip: The longer the tea sits, the stronger it will be.

Tip: If immediately icing tea, use 2 more teabags and remove lid to cool for 10-20 minutes to ensure full flavour.

NON ALCOHOLIC APPLE PEAR CIDER

Serves 4

4 apples, quartered, seeds and core removed
4 pears, quartered, seeds and core removed
2 inch piece of ginger
2 cinnamon sticks
1 lemon, quartered
1 banana, halved
80g maple syrup
Water

1. Put everything except maple syrup into pot. Add water to ⅔ full in your pressure cooker pot. I've changed this (and other recipe) to 2/3rds full according to IP manual about max levels under pressure)

2. Cook at high pressure for 25 minutes, allow pressure to naturally release for 10 minutes, then manually release.

3. Remove the lemon, ginger, and banana pieces and discard. Mash the rest of fruit until nearly pureed.

4. Cook on high pressure for 25 minutes more. Natural release.

5. Strain through a sieve

6. Stir in maple syrup whilst still warm.

Tip: This makes a tangy cider. If you prefer a sweeter cider, leave out the lemon and add more maple (or honey).

Tip: The banana provides a healthy sweetness but it does not keep as well as other fruits. If you are planning to store for more than three days, leave out the banana.

EGGNOG

Serves 4

4 medium eggs
100g sugar
330ml milk
1 tsp vanilla extract
½ tsp allspice
300ml double cream

1. Rinse inner pot with cold water. Drain out the water, but leave the pot wet. This helps prevent sticking.

2. Whisk the eggs in a bowl until smooth.

3. Add sugar and milk to eggs. Whisk until sugar is mostly dissolved.

4. Transfer egg mixture into inner pot. Press "Yogurt" and "Adjust" until "Boil" appears. Allow to boil in pot until "boil" disappears from display (approximately 20 minutes).

5. Pour the egg mixture through a sieve/mesh bag. Use a spatula to gently work the egg that has "cooked" through the mesh

6. Stir in vanilla extract, allspice, and heavy cream.

7. Chill overnight.

SAUCES & DIPS

TOMATO PASTA SAUCE

Makes about 1.3kg sauce/1.25litres

1.5kg vine ripened tomatoes
2 tbsp olive oil
1tbsp tomato puree
1 medium onion, chopped
1 red pepper, chopped
3 cloves garlic, crushed
2tbsp white wine vinegar (or your choice of vinegar)
1 bay leaf
1 tsp brown sugar
2 tsp mixed dried herbs
125ml water
Salt and pepper to season

You Will Also Need: Sterilised jars to store sauce.

1. Remove the skins from the tomatoes by scoring a cross on the base of each one and putting them in boiling water for about 30 seconds. Rinse in cold water and peel the skin off and quarter. Remove the seeds from each tomato. Cut the flesh of the tomatoes up and set to one side.

2. Heat the oil in the pressure cooker pot and gently sauté the onion and garlic until soft, about 4 to 5 minutes. Add the pepper, tomatoes and herbs and continue to sauté for a further minute or two.

3. Add the water and allow the mixture to come to a boil.

4. Set to cook at high pressure for 8 minutes and allow the pressure to release naturally.

5. Add the sugar and vinegar and allow the sauce to simmer gently for 10 to 15 minutes, or until the sauce has thickened.

6. Remove bay leaf.

7. Taste and add seasoning if required.

8. Optional: Blend to make a smooth sauce.

Serving Suggestion: Stir into cooked pasta. See the <u>Penne Pasta in Tomato Sauce</u> recipe.

BROCCOLI ALFREDO SAUCE

Serves 4

110g unsalted butter
2 cloves garlic, minced
¼ tsp salt
¼ tsp pepper
30g broccoli florets, chopped small
60ml chicken or vegetable stock
120ml double cream
120g parmesan cheese, grated
60g mozzarella cheese, grated (optional)

1. Add butter and garlic to pressure cooker pot. Gently sauté until butter melts and garlic starts to soften.

2. Add salt, pepper, broccoli and stock to pot. Set on high pressure for 0 minutes. Allow pressure to release naturally for 5 minutes.

3. Whilst the pot is still on warm, add the cream to pot, gently stirring as it warms. Add parmesan to pot, stirring as it melts.

Tip: If you want a thicker sauce, you can use mozzarella to thicken. Flour or cornstarch will also thicken thin alfredo sauce.

THAI SWEET CHILLI SAUCE

Serves 6-8

170g sugar
100ml rice vinegar (apple cider vinegar works)
60ml water
1 clove garlic, crushed
1 tbsp dried red pepper, crushed
1 tbsp flour
½ tbsp.soy sauce

1. Add sugar, vinegar, and water to inner pot. Gently sauté until the sugar has dissolved.

2. Add garlic and pepper, whisk.

3. Pressure cook on high for 10 minutes and then allow pressure to release naturally.

4. Add soy sauce and whisk in flour once removed from heat.

Tip: If serving over meat, meat can be cooked directly in sauce, and cooking time should be until meat is done.

FOUR PEPPER HOT SAUCE

NOTE: When cooking hot peppers in pressure cooker, the pepper steam cooks up very strong (it's basically pepper spray), so use extreme caution when handling peppers and removing lid of pressure cooker.

Makes about 300ml

250g jalapenos (or your choice of fresh peppers), stems removed and chopped
3 dried chilli peppers, crushed
2 garlic cloves, crushed
2 spring onions, cut to fit in pot
½ tsp ground cayenne
½ tsp black pepper (or 4-5 peppercorns)
2-3 tsp salt
180ml white vinegar
180ml apple cider vinegar

1. Add all ingredients to pot.

2. Cook high pressure 2 minutes and natural pressure release.

3. Remove lid with steam directed away from you. Do not inhale the steam.

4. Pour all ingredients into blender, or use inversion blender to puree in pot. Strain sauce through mesh and bottle.

HOT HONEY BARBECUE SAUCE

Serves 4

1 tbsp olive oil
170g tomato paste
2 tbsp honey
3 tbsp apple cider vinegar
1 tbsp molasses
¼ tsp ground cloves
¼ tsp garlic powder
¼ tsp cinnamon
Pinch ground cayenne
120ml water

1. Put olive oil, tomato paste, honey, vinegar, and molasses into pot. Whisk together thoroughly.

2. Add all spices to a small bowl and mix together.

3. Sprinkle spices into pot. Pour in water, and carefully mix until well blended.

4. Cook on high pressure for 3 minutes, and natural pressure release.

Tip: This sauce is for use in a pressure cooker. If using on a grill, use a higher smoke point oil.

Tip: If making meat in pressure cooker, meat can be cooked in the sauce until the meat is fully done.

BEETROOT DIP

Serves 4

2 raw beetroots, peeled
8tbsp cream cheese
1tbsp balsamic vinegar

You Will Also Need: Trivet

1. Put 1 cup of water in pot and the 2 raw beetroots on a trivet.

2. Cook on high pressure for 30 minutes, and gently release pressure. Water will be red and can stain, so be careful when releasing not to get steam on cabinets or counters.

3. Remove beetroot and trivet, drain away the water, and return the beetroots to the warm pot.

4. Mash the beetroot with a potato masher until just lumpy.

5. Add the cream cheese to the warm beetroots and stir until melted.

6. Mix in the balsamic vinegar.

Tip: If you prefer a smoother dip, you can use an immersion blender to remove chunks.

QUESO

1 tbsp olive oil
4 garlic cloves, crushed
40g chopped onion
40g chopped jalapenos
1 dried chilli, crushed
130g fresh tomatoes, chopped (leave in juice)
2 tbsp water
185g cream cheese
185g Mexican blend cheese, shredded

1. Sauté garlic, onion, jalapenos, and chilli in oil until tender (about 5 minutes).

2. Add tomatoes and water to pot.

3. Cook at high pressure for 2 minutes, and quick pressure release.

4. Stir in the cream cheese and Mexican cheese whilst still on warm.

THANKS FOR READING & FREE BOOKS

Dear Reader,

I really hope that you have enjoyed the recipes in this book.

If you have found this book useful I would **really** appreciate it if you could spare a moment please to leave a review on Amazon.

It really inspires and encourages me to keep on creating books. If you have any suggestions or questions please do feel free to get in contact with me at liana@lianaskitchen.co.uk

If you have any pressure cooker recipe suggestions, I would love to hear from you too!

Whenever I publish a new book on Kindle I always give it away for free (only for a few days!) If you want to find out when a new book is released, you can sign up to my VIP list right here;

www.lianaskitchen.co.uk/VIP

Happy Pressure Cooking!

Liana x